PARMENIDES IN MINNEAPOLIS

Ἵπποι ταί με φέρουσιν, ὅσον τ' ἐπὶ θυμὸς ἱκάνοι,
πέμπον, ἐπεί μ' ἐς ὁδὸν βῆσαν πολύφημον ἄγουσαι
δαίμονος, ἣ κατὰ πάντ' ἄστη φέρει εἰδότα φῶτα·
τῇ φερόμην· τῇ γάρ με πολύφραστοι φέρον ἵπποι
ἅρμα τιταίνουσαι, κοῦραι δ' ὁδὸν ἡγεμόνευον.

Parmenides of Elea

PARMENIDES IN MINNEAPOLIS

*

HENRY GOULD

Minneapolis
2025

Parmenides in Minneapolis, by Henry Gould
© Contubernales Books 2025

ISBN: 978-1-961822-21-4

*

The author gratefully acknowledges prior
publication of the title poem ("Parmenides in
Minneapolis") in *The Orphic Review*.

Front cover : shaggy ink cap mushroom

Back cover : pen-&-ink drawing by Mary Ravlin
Gould [ca. 1963]

TABLE OF CONTENTS

Part I. Parmenides in Minneapolis

Part II. The Gold Ring

Part III. The Grail

I

Parmenides in Minneapolis

PARMENIDES IN MINNEAPOLIS

The night may come as no surprise, Parmenides.
Unhurried elongations of a May evening
foreshadow, in the limbs of trees
your final chariot-ride, to the beginning
from the end (some unforeseen antipodes).
O Goddess – my nightmares, your horses!
The evening star lingers for days like these :
soft, subtle-erupting aftershocks of everything.
Time, marshal all your dull forces! So
my heart is kindled (toward a green Hesperides).

So it seems our history, my Greeks, my friends,
is an epic of disillusionment. There are the gods,
there are we humans... and never the twain blends.
A sadness seeps into our streets. What are the odds
of immortality? *Keep ever to the right,*
murmur the golden tablets in Gravesend –
that white willow, lethal, leads not to goldenrods.
O lucid firefly... from your immeasurable height
breathe out your sweet *agape* – bridge our amends!

The star glows, intermittent. Over the noise.
Phoebe, mother-child, today was your birthday.
Now night descends on you (Sophie, also). Skies
dim. Stars rise. It's Minnesota's birthday, too –
the new flag flies. The *North Star* state.
Loons yodel, on their way to Paradise –
like poets do. Parmenides, Dante...
hope against hope. Muttering (in solitaire)... *create.*
One limpid spring, one aquifer. Whispers – *surprise.*

5.11.24

S.S. NORMANDIE

The white sand stretches across a bright firm line
like a carpenter's level. Our landing craft bobs,
a seasick drunk, weaving, off-plumb. Fine :
we'll get there (dead or alive). The corporal sobs.
He sees it coming – this hollowness in the gut
you can't avoid. Life! No longer me and mine.
Becomes duel of inhuman force, driving blind mobs
to stuff the Reichstag of a power-mad puppet.
So we wade ashore at Normandy, to bring him down.

The nickname for the *Constitution* was *Old Ironsides*.
Some say the invention of democracy
emerged from Doric iron of Greek brotherhoods;
when sharing out the take, kings meant hypocrisy.
But the current of an equal sign sinks deeper yet.
This unison is no consortium of human prides –
rather a radiant consort, like *S.S. Normandie*.
War came. She burned, after molting to *U.S. Lafayette*.
In Pinelawn Memorial, her *psyche*-soul (*La Paix*) resides.

In the beginning was the unknown soldier. Anonymous
Norman, buried with the dragon-ship. Elusive
maquise de la Résistance (femme courageuse).
Each water droplet threads that metal sieve,
and every soul stands in your misty lamplight,
Dieu (and murmurs, *Yes*). Stony geometry answers,
just so. So Boethius and Thierry believe –
the universal grey of Everyman congeals at Chartres.
Love comes as servant to the commonweal (to heal, to
                                        bless).
                                                    6.6.24

8

ON FLAG DAY

Ensconced in octagon-gazebo, of cedar made
and of mosquito net, grown more and more
askew, warped, age-lined and decayed
as I wax ancient, more decrepit and heart-sore...
– I *did* remember to hang out the flag today !
The banner that droops like heat-soaked marmalade
at the stern of *Old Ironsides*, in Boston Harbor –
U.S.S. *S.O.S.*, miming *Emergency – Send Aid* :
brass emblem for a wobbly *Constitution* (made, unmade).

Under the authority of Time, it seems
all things disintegrate back to their elements.
The blue-black, starry sky; white reams
of ailing corn, papering the red-brown tents
of Martian clay... What planet, then, are we?
The red white blue shed green black orange beams;
revenge, reversals – scandal, punishments...
gray mist over blue graveyard. Can you see?
The bull's-eye of a shipwright's level... closes. Dreams.

God looks into the heart; only the heart sees God.
Your bark, tall cottonwood, is lighter than feather,
puffball... floating down so slowly, riverward.
And our Ionian microcosm is a kind of weather
in the soul : this earth, this rain, these livid storms.
Black Elk or Unknown Soldier – melancholy, even-odd –
clings to the horse's reins, leans to her clover tether;
waits on his Queequeg casket for her lucky charms.
This pitch-black diamond (willows to almond rod).

6.14.24

9

THE OTHER HENRY

Henry, the other Henry, Minneapolis Henry –
ever the poet – sporting his corn-green loon t-shirt
for old mad faery Father's Day (courtesy
of bright Sophie & Phoebe) is maybe falling apart
(lovely). & Alexander is painting the town
out there in Portland, OR (literally)... *don't talk to me
about that*, Gimoozaabi. You doppelgänger, she hurt
like lightning. Locker room mystery (gettin' me down).
A' goes on board, arguing to London. *Be? Not be?*

Zen rocks in the sand, in Kyoto. Icons of calm.
Or Yuki the cat, kicking around my absent wine-cork
(hockey equilibrium, incarnate). *Is there no balm
in Gilead?* There is. But... life is not joke.
There's Providence in sway of yarrow (gravitational)
& in Romanian 3-spheres, a single point off the beam
folds random origami, all the way to New York.
Your canoe became an oval galley, very educational
& I rigged a toy *Constitution*, in 1964 (basement rec room).

In the *Aeon of the Fox*, folks, fraud will thrive
on strife. And yet we live within a curved-sphere
mirror-cosmos (closed). *Seek ye the Lord and live*
counsels the dome on Morris Avenue : your
                                    doppelgänger's
here. Your brother, sister... mother, neighbor... you,
                                    yourself.
So fold papyrus around one golden mote of this beehive –
each soulful private is a man-door, *là* (curled in your ear).
Jiminy Cricket – Frisbee – miniature emerald elf...
crossing Poe's titanium eddy-vortex. Here you arrive.

CAUTANTOWWIT

Juneteenth. Evening was ripe and peaceful here
today. Emancipation for the soul
a simple civic ritual (*All Clear*).
Self-effacing, unassuming. Dignity, for all –
sovereign benevolence of liberty, under the law.
Room for every eccentricity : *What cheer,
Netop?* Cusa is playing chunkey-ball
with Canonicus... and out of the jaw-
bone of Death, knocked back on his heels, here comes
austere

Achilles himself! Out of the grave he's bearing
bundles of meadow weeds, for his wounded heroes –
boys, pierced with yellow arrows. The gold ring
(a thousand green brainstems, on white cloud) goes
for their damaged collateral. It's a power game
for musty, fizzled men (a traditional thing,
a mental habit : *kill your enemy*). Blood flows...
everything flows, intones the sage (blind, lame).
Yet our hearts burned at his funeral (Canonicus,
ætheling).

Minneapolis cops traveled to New Haven for the service.
Jamal Mitchell, a very good young man, fallen
in the line of duty. So the *circle of John* is
remembering that *Son of Joy* to this very day : one
unforgettable person stands in (for the neighborhood).
You know her : she's your mother, she's your father's
wife... brother, sister. *Hurt is such a one.*
The air is soft tonight; it is the common good.
Yarrow is sweet... an healing herb (*Cautantowwit's*).

HURRICANE BERYL

Hurricane Beryl now careens toward Yucatan
flashing ominous and sickly green (pink,
violet, orange)… weaving, serpentine
toward Mayan hamlets, ruins. Cusa, think
again : here's your erratic clay ballgame
grown ineluctable sea-monster; a bull (Minoan)
borne by wind, whose fatal salt we drink
within his labyrinth of all ill-fame –
Parmenides' four horses, thrown by the sun.

The orbit of every fable is double, this way –
some folded ellipse of storm-tossed paper
wraps itself around a single cyclone eye.
Mast turns to stone on sea-bottom, sailor
whose creeping horizontal coral syntax
molds bones into a seashell catafalque (*hey
ey yo*) – far glinting burial for Little Bear.
Scary gold scarab, sealed in amber wax
like Alexander in his Alexandria (*auto-da-fé*).

So this is poetry, Parmenides!
Locked room, or cognitive nightmare?
That storm comes thundering across the seas
like ten freight trains (they could be anywhere
tonight, along these wide Sargasso plains). Indeed,
America. The poison plant is in its seeds.
Ishmael, on coffin, cries – *Fresh air!*
Poe ponders his eureka – *Life's high meed.*
Your son's inside – is home, elliptical Ulysses.

6.29.24

12

FIRECRACKERS

July is here – another birthday for the nation.
The yoke of a remote king and his armies we
cast off... firecrackers (freedom's recreation).
For crowned prerogatives there's no immunity.
We shall not bend the knee. Only Law is King
where human dignity is justice, power's reason –
happiness, harvest of solidarity.
From every mountainside, let freedom ring.
Oh, if only it were so! Pike's Peak's an oven.

My country is a mystery to me.
Of power. Triple-threaded knot : a noose
of Union, Concord, and Equality.
And money. Liberty, let loose
by chance – *good fortune rides on enterprise.*
Mark Twain lights a cigar, a thoughtful Yankee
in Connecticut... Abe Lincoln's in caboose.
His end (and Camelot's) is no surprise.
Que LA PAIX, d'Alph à Barataria à Point Reyes... BE.

How to be a good Greek? That oven bird is fiery –
querulous, tonight. I'll walk into the woods
with you, Hobo. One round red berry,
equal from every angle, is Ravenna's good;
from your elliptical *two* emerges *one*,
sweet-scented Giuliana – mossy pine-faery...
my languor's mumbling now (by Mississippi).
Of love and wilderness, these are the wounds,
Aphrodite, murmurs Empedocles. *Love is mighty.*

7.1.24

ODYSSEUS

These ancient weathered lips still keep the shape
of a bronze horseshoe, or just a single sandal
flung like a leftover, down Etna slope –
faint footprint from some lost idyll,
forgotten scandal. Here, under febrile cedar
of dried-out gazebo, shuddering like crepe,
an oven bird sweeps clean her upturned bowl.
It's empty now. Fled is her family choir.
Only chattering echoes cannot escape

these fields of doom. Yet the puzzle is a breeze!
Perplexes her solitude. Like a shadow, whispering
behind a door – a zero Someone, in disguise –
lightweight, ungraspable. Memoir of something
sweet and simple as a yellow yarrow bloom,
that sways on its stem in wide, forsaken meadows
as balm for Achilles' wounds, easing their sting.
Hovering, honeybees buzz and zoom.
Earth's requiem soars (above its mortal frieze).

Her heart is calling you. Insistent as boomerang
or monotone cicada – calling your heart of stone
to open, like a feathered wing. Just so, she sang.
And you saw the oven of the sun fold round and burn
an oblong diaphragm – Venn diagram.
It was mandala to her chamber... Everything;
bright cloud of oneness, flared from spheric Union.
This knot – this mutual equality – is truth, not sham!
Your Whisperer... is home. Arrows subdue Time's fang.

7.3.24

VERSES FOR THE FOURTH OF JULY

"That's the teaching of Jesus. Pretty hard, ain't it? That's
what He did. He suffered on that cross for prostitutes – not for saints,
not for the good guys. Go on – give away your farm to the first bum
you see on the street, or the prostitute in some bar… pretty crazy,
huh? 'That guy's nuts!' Can't you hear the voices? Oh yeah, all
them good guys… But that's what Jesus did."
                    – Father Finughan (quoted in *Old Glory*, by Jonathan Raban)*

In this unjust and wormwood midnight of a world
blind Man-Woe might nevertheless bear inborn
compass. Some magnetic north, purled
half-true and mesmerized, around her twin –
the double matrix of an oblong egg.
Platonic memory of perfect form; unfurled
like my green shamrock years in Mendelssohn
(that fiddler's neighborhood). Blind man, I beg.
Heart-channels, breathing sighs (to wombward, curled).

We dwell in a curved and finite universe
outside whose swelling gunwales not even nothing
swims : our sun, our stars and galaxies
we scry through an inward glass (an oblong ring,
a mirror). Poe, with his locked-room mystery

encrypted himself. *Bury My Heart at Wounded Knee*
keens on the wind of Black Elk's people-mourning,
turns each scar in the heart toward *Old Glory* –
each soul a microcosm of Black Hills (pining).
Soft Evening Star, *above high plains*… heal my verse.

This oval ark of the dignity of a microcosm
is the binding law of human Union. We are *Imago*

of the Perfect : bent rays toward the bosom
of your vanishing point, Persephone (*Shekinah*).
The blind man cannot see, except the heart
sees everything already. Old men dream
a prophecy – your golden tablets, Prospero;
your *New World* (cosmic Kid's new start).
Under the gutless, hulking Bull... bees hum.

7.4.24

Old Glory : a voyage down the Mississippi, by Jonathan Raban,
©1981; from first Vintage Departures edition, Vintage Books,
1998, p.134.

SUMMER HORSES

A stone fell from heaven... or was it apple from a tree?
Your neighbor-child, in the deep backlands
heard it fall, far off... too far to see.
Listen... *you must retreat from Time's demands*
sometimes, the grass whispered. Psyche, or stone?
World is swallowed up in forgetfulness, Parmenides,
murmured his Queen of Mares. *The* One *is quicksand* :
still, clear, motionless. You kings at Scone,
hearken to Roma woman : rest in Reality.

And so I traced my sister-comet, my royal diadem,
on her elliptical path above a summer meadow.
Like iridescent firefly track, or milky gem –
marking the rim of some enormous oval scow
or winking galley-dhou... the Ark? *Old Ironsides*?
Primordial ship (beyond Athens, Rome, Jerusalem)
her chariot floated in that sea of grass – and now
her horses come to nudge me... her Nereids.
No one is alone, Parmenides. So follow them.

You hear me whispering, out of the ground.
Like some riddling inscription on a gold tomb-
tablet – your ear already in the burial-mound
of horses, kings... (among slaves there's room
for you, as well). Each humble person is a soul.
I looked in the graves, Mother – you I never found;
I listened by the stones, Father – but your hymn
was gone. Somewhere each person rises, whole
and sound... and sounds. Hear *Ocean* roll.

7.13.24

17

ET LA VIE EST FACILE

My oriole sings out of the heart of summer,
out of the solar plexus of *la joie-de-vivre*.
She was born to chant, it is of her nature –
like Seine that flows between Bastille and Louvre.
Aie me! My memories are lost at sea.
The oven bird immures himself, a cinder
in the forest gloom – only an ember's flare.
Aie me! My memories are lost at sea;
heart carols (corals) what mind would remember.

There is a little watercolor Grandma daubed
in high school (Iowa City). A soft brown
ectoplasmic mist... no, that's not right (fobbed
off the internet). Thin steeple, sown
like wheat beside calm West Branch stream.
Out of vast open sky, prairie (robbed
near Spirit Lake – hid in storm cellar, someone
said)... like wheat beside a West Branch stream.
Old bigots rock on Quaker porch – rifled, cobwebbed.

O querulous mind, Empedocles!
From Uncle Jim, Grandma's grand sailor boy –
served on a battleship (censored the news)
off Guam – his own mail home a Joycean joy...
Aie me! My memories are lost at sea.
Strife and Love... Hades and Aphrodite...
such is life, in this world of sharp foils
and foolish words! *Aie me, aie me...*
aye-aye. My prairie evening (orioles are memory).

7.14.24

CATALPA

The riffling spinnaker of the catalpa
strains its great mass against the breeze.
Soft evening air. Here, at the alpha
of its midpoint apex : a basket of eggs.
St. Swithin heard that widow's anguished cry
upon a bridge in Winchester – and lo (*abra*
cadabra) his touch restored frail promises
of Easter. So air swathes leaves... they sway
my heart that way : a reflex memory (*selah*).

He is an old man... (Malcolm's *matryoshka*)
and now I will never see him again. Seize
the day (it's Henry's, too) – Bonaventure,
seraph-docteur... even you, Parmenides –
stern yearner! It's just – a gust of air.
A street in Paris, where you skipped, Dora,
shrouded in crowds (a leaf among leaves).
My *Shulamit*, your dark black hair –
each circle urges into oval, so (*duend-aya*).

Not infinite, the universe. Comes to a close.
Yet there is no perimeter, no cage.
Dante beheld a double wreath, of rose –
heaviness, tenderness... *la tendresse attristée.*
Rage, rage, against the dying... everywhere.
You'll see : that circle is familiar face –
it has no edge, but smiles. Across the stage
great waves of blue crash – cold, stark terror!
Yet your almond bow skims in, secure. Harbors.

7.15.24

ATLANTIS BLUE

The air of summer seeps into your veins,
somehow. Light breeze out of a broken crystal,
bright, invisible. And yet these bloodstains
will not wash away : and that is all.
Indelible. In shade of Popocatepetl
Jacques Laruelle remembers Chartres; those panes
of bleeding rainbow light; how the Consul
asked to be buried with Blackstone. O subtle
mystery of disaffection! Juniper Yvonne remains.

Young hawks interrogate each other now
up in the arbor vitae, outside this gazebo.
They're playing, hunting. Elliptical, your *Ludo
Globi*, Nicolas, Blackstone – somehow
I've tripped, and fallen from perfection.
And yet, by Keats, I will distend this O
into a negative oblong – swan-dive off bow
to hellfire (Hades, Hecate, Poseidon!) –
mold a beehive on Charon's sticky prow.

Aya! Seraph-docteur, Bonaventure…
your cemetery haunts me, in Savannah.
The live-oaks whisper through an aperture
in time – where friendly faces gleam. *Hosannah.*
Now you may mime the monarch butterfly;
out of her leaden plummet of infernal sulfur,
rise – a fey, faery Yvonne (Psyche, Ophelia).
Your coracle's become canoe. An oval mandorla.
Lost summer's keep, Atlantis blue (*Deep River*).

7.17.24

20

DOVES REHEARSE

A breeze penetrates this broad-beamed catalpa
like sound of the sea. And through the feeble mesh
of twine speech-gazebo, the same salty Alph
abets my voyage to *Quauhnahuac* (like Gilgamesh,
or Ahab). My heart, my friend... *dark is the grave.*
Plummets toward Tartarean fire – like Atahualpa
on a gold doubloon; my prayers are but vain wish
amid such snow-drop Poe designs. *Breeze, lave
my soul! Tender your leafy whisper*, Perdita.

My song is but a weakling scree, with ballast
of bombast. It cannot heal, or save.
My cratered heart sheers due southwest,
led by *Cautantowwit*; crows hector, vultures rave
where monarchs bangle their deep cedar nest.
O Plotinus, your One is past all mind, number :
your circle swells, elliptical, into a wave
whose love resolves our yearning into wonder :
that far goldfinch, to yarrow firefly (at last).

So this locked room of Poe's eureka universe
explodes with the singular volcanic-Etna power
of *Union* itself. The One that is the Many's nurse
and throws (like Pip, like Hobo, Unknown Soldier)
across to Huck, a Thief between two thieves –
a floating human (Everywoman, Everyman) whose face
you faintly recognize... you've seen before.
Tears flow like rain... beyond what mind conceives
Coulombe conceives. Love keens... where doves rehearse.

7.22.24

OUTSIDE NEW HAVEN

Edgar, restless nightingale, buries a beak
in his scryptorium. Over the doorway, Raven
creaks – *Cautantowwit* (southwest, southwest). Reek
of ancient sacrifice. Outside New Haven
Orpheus plunges through a wormhole, to Taranto;
those golden burial tablets that you seek
are sown like wheat, blown everywhere (ghostwritten).
Kid, thou art fallen into milk... Simone Weil. So.
Apocrypha from *Opus Posthumous*. Earth, for the meek.

The ruthless pendulum of time keeps circling,
as if to mock the innocence of children
soon grown old. Envious clock, still lurking!
Tapping the ticking seconds of each hand... *my son,
my son*. Nothing can stall my sleepwalking.
Are souls gathering underground, or hurtling
into the sky? What can save this trembling man
from his own melancholy? Mind, cease talking.
Nightingale is numbering. Soft (darkness; whistling).

Parmenides was haunted by four nightmares
of apocalypse. Flesh torn from spirit,
flung to abstract, scripted Dreamtime – terrors
of the Absolute. And of the heart's deceit,
mind's vanity, there's something to be said.
Still, Orpheus awaits faint far-off choirs...
Psyche, Jonah... two voices, one heartbeat –
and suddenly the hypersphere lifts from seabed.
Our loved ones live forever. Dove's not dead.

7.23.24

SOMEDAY

Your air, July, is fathom-full of humid sea.
Remember, how her ship sank in the grass?
Her bark, her cedar coracle, was lost to me.
All hands. Eight bells. Roll of the dice.
Jonah, tossed off Mobile, met the whale
that way. Vast ribs groan... sonorously.
You slept, sailor – become both prophet and loess.
Flotsam. Splinter. Threadbare, discount sail.
In long salt wake, gray olive twig... (like wingèd V).

In blue-green Pineland – a quiet cemetery
up beyond Big Apple's grave shipyards –
all that remains of *S.S. Normandie*
remains. *La Paix* – a tiny *Liberté* – she guards
the pathway back to dry land, like an aqualung;
Man's lies seem fathomless – or only a story
Captain Hook contrives, to signal his distress.
In whom we live and move... only a bird (unsung).
Hermione's pigeon, with message : *Land Ho*, Agape.

This green season's quiet is a mystery.
Kids are singing over there, beyond the fences.
A sweet chorale (improv, from memory).
The slow wheels of my coracle condense
two feathered paddles into one. Dark roses,
in an olive-green oblong – human storm-eye,
preternaturally calm. It's our coincidence :
what Noah opens with a raven, Jonah closes
with a smile. Hovering there, in Nineveh... someday.

7.24.24

LUCKY DEUCALION

On an ongoing wave of the sea I came ashore
drawn by both hands into a relay dance
around and around, a never-ending choir.
Life became dream, a secret semblance
of mysterious balance. As if, still at sea,
compass and tiller were in tune once more –
tilting slightly (tragedy to romance)
drowned sailors merge with coraline reality,
and contraries embrace in one sweet score.

Those golden wheat-fields of lingering pain
sway like Ulysses' memory of Ithaca;
light far-off voices trill their round again
and children – spirits, now – trace a trifecta
across the sand : running with laughter
on either hand. Mother is the prophet *Jonah*,
Father is lucky Deucalion –
no one shall die – we live forever after;
soon the deep-scarred Thief returns... to reign.

Intransigence is just a shade of faith
and groans, the daily birthing-pangs of hope;
when love lifted Parmenides (a wraith
full of nightmares) he saw the sunny envelope
around Penelope, round Aphrodite... like a face
full of light, beaming her *Argo* on its path –
like an Ark above Paris, Constantinople.
Dark hair, dark eyes, round olive-almond grace.
Dancer from Magdala... turning your lathe.

7.26.24

LOVE YOUR NEIGHBOR AS YOURSELF

The young gymnast tumbles, somersaults, and leaps
into thin air – for a moment hovering aloft
on nothing at all. And those bridges Paris keeps
suffused all night with rain-blows... and the soft
whisper of the Seine, bearing her singing barges
filled with Olympic champions... Overhead sweeps
the ark of Notre Dame. And I recall another craft
of Greek invention : how geometry forges, enlarges
Manna *(pain)* from ineffable *One* (Parmenidean steeps).

Hugging his wintry hill of Chartres, Thierry would frame
equations chalked from haunted, pre-Socratic oracles
to reconcile *Logos* and *Numeros*, Jerusalem
and Athens : on those almonds drift our coracles.
Then mystic Nicolas of Cusa (in *De Ludo Globi*)
sketched a proposal for the Game of Games –
come out and play! The cenacle of cenacles
is everyone's, who will – *Dribble and see*!
The ball twirls in your inner ear, brawny St. James.

Edgar Poe, in his locked-room mystery
sent a rabid orangutan across Paris.
We are each inimitable individuals, see –
sealed in permafrost; there's no comparison.
Yet that greater *One* looms – like Penelope
a threaded Unity, deeper than Ocean Sea;
borne on such *Argo* solidarity, nothing scares us.
Cusa's ball is Dante's hypersphere – reality
is : *Ve'ahavta le'reyakha kamokha*. Justice, mercy.

7.27.24

CAPE GOOD HOPE

This sultry summer air... doldrums, dog days.
Stasis, stillness. The ropes are slack. Canvas
hangs limp. The shore exudes a filmy haze
of seaweed memory. Where's my taut windlass
now? To draw me down and anchor me
(like salt) to veritable ocean floor?
Soon night will fall. Far lightning bugs will blaze
like twinkling fleets, rounding the universe
(their *Cape Good Hope*). Heart canna see nae more.

Firefly, I want to hide myself in your long grass
and shed this surly skin, that led me winding
along shady paths of lechery and avarice –
all overshadowed by timidity (uncanny, binding).
I was lost in the world : lost to my proper self.
O Hecate, in your black glass of Tartarus
I scried the pinpoint of Polaris, glimmering –
past time and space, beyond desire, bland pelf.
Beyond all motion, light was shining... motionless.

The heart's a kind of bivalve coracle
anchored full-fathom to the ocean floor.
So each stout carrack is a human oracle –
like *Argo*, wisdom whistles her ashore.
The figurehead of *Loving Farther* at the bow
allows her boy to pilot from the stern (fo'c's'l
a-brim with *Chartres*... all plotted before).
Hummings in the spine inspire her now!
Love threads the keel (turtleshell miracle).

7.28.24

26

RAINBOWS ARC

Slight things, the faintest scent, provide the ballast.
Soft bump of dropping fruit; eddying pumice...
these serve for plummet-compass to the Holy Ghost.
So, Soul... be lifted back to her fledgling-nest.
Odysseus, knotted writhing to his mast
heard that untouchable Sirens' far-off grace-
note... tasted Mnemosyne's bread-crumb at last :
leaned late into the feathered ribs of Jonah's breast.
And shattered, sinking *Pequod*... only a harpoon-cast.

The retired ship-captain sleeps in his still gazebo
across the long afternoon. And of Jerusalem
heavy Henry dreams. High-hearted (long ago).
Those lambent, darting lamps of Byzantium
are crepuscular gold bars now, foiled in lead –
his chamber only a locked room, sealed by woe.
Only a rusted compass still points straight to Him
who lifts the spirit with pure fire : *life to the dead,*
sounds her sweet requiem (violets, Io).

You hear the humming of the lightweight bees
above my bull's crashed hull. Like attainted Papa
in his small room, move slowly through these lees
on one light breeze – one sigh of *eucharistia.*
Give thanks : this is the Sabbath that God sees.
Behind the arras and the rustling ornaments
your humble father meets his Prodigal –
my son, my son. Heart's inner sanctum harbors
peace. And rainbows arc through all realities.

7.29.24

YOUR BANNER OVER ME

Sophie and I designed an entry for the Flag Contest –
fashioned to coax contrary town and country folks
to join together in one governing Waltz. The best
was somebody else's, yet our homemade sail still floats
above the front door – our own private Minnesota.
There's a big North Star, lofted northwest,
and 32 bright little ones, like river-motes
below the Falls – Mississippi's first and last hurrah;
also one shady purple oval (underneath a Norway spruce).

Such banners often flag us into war.
Strife is of the essence, squawks Empedocles.
All men are blind. How still the stones are!
– sez intransigent Parmenides.
Visible – invisible; life – death;
mortal humanity... bright gods, immortal;
evil... righteousness... Strife sees.
One infinitesimal gold earring spins – on a breath
of metaphysical spring (Aphrodite's answer).

Vanity of vanities... all men are blind.
Like fearful flocks they fly into the nets;
like heartless sharks they terrorize their kind;
like devious snakes they harness life to bets –
and all these melodramas, horror shows
are merely pantomimes of that impenetrable knot,
that *fleur du mal*, in every human heart and mind!
Life seamed with shame... Strife sees, Strife knows.
These garish banners, locked in hate! Who can unbind?

Between the Tree of Knowledge and the Tree of Life,
fused at their roots, like a poplar family
stands the supple Tree of Wisdom, wearing a coif
of laurel. That's your Greek name, Sophie.
A garland of intertwining leaves around your head
configures (with geometry's rough knife)
the seamless fabric of reality :
incomprehensible close weave. The dead,
the living, here, are one, in love... husband and wife.

My muddled mellifluousness cannot bring to pass
a benevolent future (or present, or past).
Cicadas drone in their cottonwood crevasse,
while Time surges on, downstream... we are aghast
at our ephemeral state. Changes in the weather
throw us on the mercy of a clown's *diktat*,
who slurps his doomfields from a china demitasse.
O, who shall save us? We must work together!
That hero – *Unknown Soldier* – is the human race!

Now serious thunder booms outside my writerly gazebo.
The judgements of the LORD *are true and righteous
altogether*. Amen, bro. Let it be so.
All flesh is grass-fed beef. Let there be no noxious
odors in the sanctuary of this typewriter.
Body (everybody) torn from soul, someday – oh
Lord... and must it come to that? Oh yes.
Aphrodite, Zeus... somebody phoning Hecate? Oh sure.
In the black mirror of Black Elk (hovers a light zero).

And in a moss-green, spring prairie, I entered the ring
of blessèd names, of affectionate spirits;
in the oval coracle of lost souls – remembering,

being found again, like orphan *Cautantowwits* –
the ravens from the Ark came back again
accompanied by one grey-violet *coulombe* (unknown)
who gripped a laurel twig, broken to bits (almost).
She placed it on the bow... a grain of wheat, sown
long before. Psyche, Persephone... Miriam, singing.

Odysseus listened. He had left the boat
already – overboard, into the salt. *Thalassa...*
Ishmael, Jonah. Old mariner (his every groat,
his every scar, measured). As at Itasca
dewdrops on jewel-weed merge with the spring,
he sank... one of the patients of the patient
Earth. All sin is from *cupiditas*, alas...
impatience is a feverish unknowing –
is our present being. *Ingrates, all*. Fleas, float!

I will go stand by the poor man at the harbor,
down by the docks. I will go sit with his mother,
begging on the banks. I will enter his old arbor,
and lie down under the shade of that green poplar,
and cry my fill of tears, for the woe that is in me.
And then I will look to the sky, toward your North Star,
Sophie. And at last I will begin to remember
the joy that surges from that light, perennially;
and I will listen for you, Dove – your soft whisper.

                                            7.31.24

THE GOOD RAIN

The good rain falls on the first day of August
and the little pinecone canoes drift down the street
threading their Alph, their Nile, down to the Gulf Coast,
to the grand old Sea, her deep moon-wave heartbeat.
And I hear a grey dove, fluting her Sabbath day.
In our time, when evils fester as they must,
that undertone, her melody beneath our feet
recalls us to our peace. So let us pray
for an innocent child-heart : find what was lost.

The grey stone that floated down from the sky
lighter than pumice, sweeter than a plum
became the river-pilot's plummet, and the eye
on *Argo's* bow : kind wisdom, patient, calm.
Oval in an oval, pearly-grey seashell,
whose buoyant singing fills the sails with joy –
translating souls to that concentric realm
where *all shall be well, all manner of thing shall be well.*
We inherit your cosmic commonweal... ply over ply.

A child stands before his grandmother, his grandfather
and looks them in the eye, and laughs with glee,
and spins around... and they behold him, there.
This is a *logos*-mystery, of I and Thou, of you and me –
of timeless Spirit, rooted like a tree
in trusting heart – an infant architecture,
swelling with the forest breeze of all reality.
Ineffable airs of unchanging eternity
balanced that heart-boat (justice lighter than a feather).

8.1.24

31

CONTRARY TWINS

Stalin, Akhmatova, contrary twins –
despot, poet – both died on March 5th.
20 years apart. Dialectic's void opens
in every conversation. Hollow gulf
or pregnant pause; a gap, held in suspense
between 1, and 2. Where everything begins
or ends. In these imperial dog days of 8th-
month summer dreams... all is coercion, violence.
Parmenides' *Nightmare of Sham* tears at our skins.

In my irenic '50s Minnesota childhood,
with plastic parts and airplane glue, I spent
long days in basement, doing what I could
to build a model of *Old Ironsides* (her pennant
still unfurls, in Boston Harbor). *Constitution.*
Now evil churls would have it all unscrewed,
sunk – for power and/or money... pure deceit.
Liberty, democracy, and law – to be undone.
Is *Free World* so fragile now? So wormed with fraud?

Yet perhaps Law is not a brittle plastic boat
just as *l'Eglise* is not a hulking stone carcass.
I think of Osip, living Ovid of the Soviet;
of that clear apostolic air, his meek St. Isaac's.
Verse is metamorphosis – someone leaping
from Chinese junk to junk... the rounded note
of Attic honeybees... a goldfinch on the topmast.
Maybe law is such a spry clipper – *Ariel... Taiping...*
Law, the human *St. John's Fire* : truth burning bright.

It's not Rome, the city, but Man's place in the universe.
The bond between democracy and the Real –
existence, actuality – is numbered in the stars,
grounded in human dignity : here I set my seal.
We live and die this life in one another –
word, *logos*, relation, *ratio*. Sophia sets our course.
From primal *Union* [1] emerges *Equality* [2]... now feel
the solid air of *Concord* [3]. Sister, brother...
father, mother... *ÉCU* (shielding Olympiad Paris).

I'm talking about the *Unknown Soldier* – birdlike
                              Mandelstam,
et al. Mind, heart, *esprit*. His bronze mushroom helmet
in the grass. The man-door, woman-door, *là* – the hum
of bees on the last hill, fallen down. *4th Quartet*
of Virgil (1-3-2)... *Hymn of thanksgiving to the Deity*
for my recovery from illness... and so on (amen).
The nightingale fever has not subsided yet.
Pindar is entering the horseshoe contest – ringing
bronze against iron... matching oriole's I AM.

Over the wintry heights of Chartres, the scintillating
                              peaks
of Beatrice's *ben del intelletto*, floats a homing pigeon.
Thierry and Cusa, treading back to pre-Socratics
for the quickening of the *One* (Pythagorean,
Parmenidean) – and grafting it, in brain-confusion
to that ruddy Day-Lily of Israel : who streaks
like lightning toward the tree of Golgotha, alone
(yet not alone). That unknown soldier touches everyone
with pain, with mercy – throws the eagles' justice in their
                              beaks.

I grew up in Minnesota. Family is old Twin Cities.
Twins : my father and Aunt Mary. Loneliness,
imaginary friends... a solitary soul seeks her affinities.
The circle swells, extends. Oblongs, ellipses...
far-distant water *lotos* of midwestern planet (grass-
bent plains). Your path, brainy Empedocles?
Firewater melancholy... Lowry's, Aiken's, Berryman's?
Heart's anchor spools her salty windlass
to the end : *Dark Lady* (Mary Magdalen, Hecate).

That ship's gone down, long time ago.
Some scholar's model of the *Book of J* –
Shakespearean bad mood (so Deirdre moans, Iago).
You're missing something here, Ed Poe. Aye?
Why don't you take the subway home? Dark broods
the thunderhead... just passed Chicago, now.
Heaviness, tenderness... whorled in array.
Twin sisters... roses... Dante's, Euclid's...
Albertian hypersphere, my friend. God's *Imogen*.

We never leave these Tuscan hills of Voronezh,
I-Thee, I-Thou. Your smiling glance, Nadezhdaean
flickers with evening lake-light, *maia Xhena*.
The Czar is not the Son of God – he's but a penguin
suited up for polar ice (abysmal trump, O Queen
of Spades). Let N'Orleans Mardi Gras Indians,
my voodoo chile, come testify : *I'm pretty, Man –
don't bow to nobody but God, in New Orleans.*
I hear that sea-wash... Peace. SHALOM. *Voilà la neige.*

8.1.24

34

II

The Gold Ring

THE PERIHELION

The perihelion of summer has passed by.
In the woods, wild grapes of September
scent the air. *Ripeness is all.* Goodbye,
green cornfields – greetings, honey-amber
amulets, star-flecked Ravenna tombs.
Seasonal dominion, power and glory
rise to an apex, like statue of an emperor –
yet time rolls on, into winter's close rooms.
Gargantuan beast, with almost-human face... *vale.*

Like a frowzy Noah, couched in weedy octagon
I ponder kingdoms' ends, look toward Elijah.
Parmenides would understand, my son
(Elisha too) : her quatrefoil charisma,
shady green, grows supernatural.
Burns with the heat of that intransigent man
who stumbled seasick back to Nineveh –
Jonah Rainbow-Neck (light on stone wall).
So all Authority is given... one grey urban pigeon.

One quick tense rabbit – grey, quiet – leaps
through late summer grass. Noah glances up
briefly – thinks of his brazen goats and sheeps
(twinned on the Ark). Inherently corrupt
is the Czar, apparently – all the paraphernalia
of Byzantium cannot... Death is for keeps.
Eli dropped out of nowhere, some Unknown Cop –
people clung to his word (like Abraham, or MLK).
The Sower sows, the sower sleeps... Cicada reaps.

9.9.24

THE AVOCADO

This valedictory September light
is tender, as the sun withdraws – is tenderness
itself. Transparent are the shades – off-white,
moss-green, leaf-brown. Now the cicadas
drill straight through all natural phenomena
while crowds of crickets prophesy night-
fall. Old men recall their salad days;
the mower beholds a mirage of Giuliana;
remote barn swallows launch their Rio flight.

For severe Parmenides, Truth is much like ice :
transparent, cold, more still than stone.
Our life's a travesty (not very nice)
suborned by the Unreal – what's born's undone;
such chilly fraud breeds philosophic fire.
Granddad threw a Yule log on the hearth, once, twice...
from last year's Christmas tree. The wise atone
transgressions, so that Man may not expire
from shame, but yet prevail. Hearken, Parmenides!

Solomon, in colloquy with radiant Sheba
strives to address her hard questions... meanwhile
her lizard-green frogsuit, glinting harmonica
distracts him, like a swift Nile coracle –
is she some kind of avocado? Pale moon-
orb, planted in the center of that mudpie,
heavy as the judgement of *Ja-El*...
soft, soft! Wisdom's a light pontoon!
Like some Venetian catamaran... (halleluiah).

9.11.24

AFTER HESIOD

The crickets, out in the dark, beyond the house
chorus a warning for the night to come.
Your brass shell from St.-Mihiel may not protect us,
Grandfather. Even bronze ash-men, sown in loam
are overborne by *hubris*, treachery.
Where arrogant and callous revelers carouse
grim heartbreak lurks, cold as the winter tomb.
We have sown salt into our own prairie.
Pure Strife is chief... across each homestead plows.

Gold, silver, bronze, iron : these metals
are immortal. From mountains of Zeus and Zion
they range on an unbreakable grid. Like angels,
ranked in ascending files... the doom of Man!
Cranking out our fate upon a spit of fire!
Who will deliver us from these smoking wells
of Tartarean fraud? A voice whispers : *I can.*
A human voice. Tired, caked in mire
of labor – pungent with sweat, and animals.

There is a good strife, and a bad – labor
and envy (malice). *Do not lose faith,*
friend, in the better angels of thy nature,
Abraham the trembling Quaker saith.
The little voice in the cave, who urged Elijah
to launch his immortal chariot of fire,
muttered : *break the brass shell.* That wraith
of childhood is your soul – fly free! *Selah.*
My cosmos bears you (buoyant triple sphere).

9.14.24

39

CONSTITUTION DAY

for my sister, Cara

These crickets, like the heartbeat of the earth
scrape their intrepid snares so steadily
aslant late summer's offbeat dark. Wordsworth
thumps washtub bass; Keats riffles ukelele
like the peach feathers on a sandhill crane...
they're going to harp the planet back to berth.
Athena, inside *Argo's* cedar spine, sings harmony;
her stays and rudder guide her home again
and *Gaia Cicada* drones through all her girth.

Yet winter may come. We ate the fruit
some time ago, from the Exile Tree.
Shock drills, like a greedy wasp, at the very root.
Affliction pleads, like Job : *justice, mercy*!
Yet Moby's brow remains... inscrutable.
I'll whisper-tap til midnight, like a cricket
with a trumpet, or the flute of Aphrodite.
Lights above sea-wall; compass on the table.
We'll sail ahead, though Golgotha's *en route.*

When you grow old and frail like me, unaccountably
these meek little crickets have the strongest voice.
They cannot master political reality,
or relieve our shame, or crack the iron vise
of our injustice. They can only sing.
Yet they are steadfast – straight as any keel.
So the soft heart in its ribbed casket will rejoice
despite all woe this exiled world will bring.
For the slave, whose fear is overcome, is free.

9.17.24

ELI, ELI

Late summer evening's rusty glow,
like bronze, or weathered Lebanon cedar.
Like Minnesota leavetakings, so very slow –
so lonesome (something like the sun, up there).
And when the darkness comes, it's very dark.
Old age is like a crucifixion – don't you know?
Our little life is rounded with nightmare.
Don't grouse that way! wails the vaunting lark –
'Twas in another country, long ago.

Pascal was troubled by the infinite.
Eli, Eli, lama sabachthani?
Yet strong arms ensign our wavy planet,
curved to a Reimann-manifold reality
(green clover quatrefoil, in four dimensions).
To diagram the soul takes more than wit.
Heart plummets deeper than the deep blue sea
and only light frees sunken galleons –
wide COSMOS hammocks on a grain of salt.

Don't cry, little lark... you'll be back in spring.
Your wonder shall persist beyond plain sight
– and the soul, Dante, *is an intellectual thing.*
Thus my *Dark Lady*, in the dead of night,
like a submarine coracle (russet, maroon)
taught me to yodel – *Death, where is thy sting?*
Creation's knotted, like a terabyte.
Heart bumps dock (waits for the next monsoon).
Whispers : *sail home, lost ship, from your wandering.*

9.19.24

O MY CHILD

At stern and prow, two bowlines knot
the sailor's twine, into a perfect line.
Now summer softly docks at Equinox
and Jonah, tangled in the whale's intestine
yearns like an anchor for that straightening
pull. He's time to pray and meditate,
amid the rot : Sabbath keeps him sanguine :
Union qualifies the All (beneath its spinning,
so). *Be still, my soul.* Cicada drones (*b-flat*).

The concrete words of men roll over the earth
like hordes of bartering builder-ants – assembling,
tearing down. Cheap labor? – no dearth.
All our equations solve themselves! Amazing
tautologies... instinctual tunes, untaught!
Jonah smells the swamp gas, in his clammy berth
so far from Nineveh, New York, Beijing...
what word can answer, for his trussed-up heart?
Soft, milord; 'tis but a soft word, 'sooth.

The rose of summer is fading now; the time
grows old; soon frost is at the window,
and the double knot of my familiar rhyme
will be forgot (so my tomatoes grow too slow).
I cannot help you find heaven on earth.
Heaven is heaven; Earth is earth. The *charism*
of charity comes drifting down, tomorrow –
like a feather, it will balance all your worth
upon a scale of equal tuning (*O my child of Bethlehem*).

9.21.24

GO FORTH

The fat wasp dawdles, hovering, in cedar shade
of gnarled gazebo – and with piercing soprano hum
sings as she levitates... so summer's laid
to rest. You hear the cricket tap his drum.
This quiet Friday at September's close,
the smallest sounds arise, go on parade –
oblivious to the bitter, grinding scrum,
the fraudulent sleights and threats of those
who cash their souls for the feuding cavalcade.

But what remains for us, Parmenides?
Untouchable stone – inscrutable cenotaph?
And is there no warm-hearted paradise
where goodness thrives, and happy people laugh?
The sun, the sea, the stars, the floating ship...
primordial signals on a radius
from evening Hesperides : Noah's cubit-graph,
a bottle-ship (or gleaming microchip)
for one clear, encompassing ark-universe.

Your soul's adrift now, like that sleepy wasp.
All unaware of winter... gloomy time.
A mate came to your father; and in her grasp
Earth tilted slightly, from the helm
toward the Pole Star, or magnetic North.
So the heart-gate swings, on its iron hasp
like a taut, cat-gut *chelys* string : you mime
the just tuning of the universe. Go forth,
my child, in hope : just like Nadezhda, sweet Osip.

9.27.24

SEEDLING

Now autumn dusk so swiftly turns night-dark.
I have to carry this electric lamp
out to my spindly octagon, to mark
time's hoof-prints down my hippocamp,
while waves of crickets mourn their summer sea.
So the Achaeans (waiting offshore to jump the shark)
droned their threnody... set Horse to ramp.
To compass the eight-point star of misery –
our Promethean task (since we beached the Ark).

As darkness deepens, crickets draw more close;
mime those cicadas, outside Pergamon.
The *Argo* of Apollonius Rhodos
rowed these straits... blind azure of oblivion
will not obliterate their human glory.
So what remains, O singer so morose?
I say there's a seedling of yon Eternal Person
nestled in every woman, every man – O see,
blind singer! Sniff this carnation... (cloves)!

At the nadir of Jonah's bleak and wintry well
after his defenestration from the *Argo*,
aching, into *Pontos Axeinos* – it was hell –
he noticed a green whorl, in the whale's hollow.
Something growing, like a meek mushroom
from Earth's refuse – like a wasteland spell.
Its meaning for you, I think you know.
Hope is that gray bird (Rothko's *Rainbow Room*)
adrift overhead, after the flood. *Selah*, Daniel.

9.28.24

BOWSTRING

O majestic Norway pine, reaching for the sun
like a green mast on that stony promontory
over the humble pyramid of lakeshore stone
my brother raised (forest family memory)...
your wavy flights are anchored, like the moon,
to center of the Earth. Our life – a plummet-span
down to the grave – springs in contrariety
toward Polaris. Only read the rune
etched like a taut bowstring : arc of Creation!

The wind picks up. The sky clouds over.
Elegant eagles overhead are tossed
like pontoons, lifeboats blown to cover.
It seems our dream-mandalas are embossed
in rusted iron, brass, tinsel – do not last.
Meanwhile ravens hoard Elijah's clover.
Test his fate with fire... and all his host.
Jonah (Holy Dove) leaves Man aghast –
her tongs forge fiery holocaust for Nineveh.

My brother's granite ark is a memento.
Mortal paths of rightness and honor,
sea-lanes of love and joy, remain just so.
Anchored with a knot of fire – a cinder
fused in that heart-furnace of reality.
Though all that we see will come and go,
these ashes shield an evergreen ember :
Jonah wings it with us, walking to Shiloh.

9.30.24

45

TOWARD DAYLIGHT

October's fading greens are stoked with fire
for winter : ruddy bronze and mustard gold
juxtapose, with last farewell fanfare,
their cornucopia with coming of the cold.
Your strife of opposites, Empedocles,
Parmenides, entangles Earth and Air
and Fire and Water, swirled in one clay mold
of Good and Evil... mingled parodies
of Paradise. A seasonable mire.

Nicolas of Cusa, Dean Berkeley of Eire
both leaned on Boethius to celebrate
inscapèd power of the mind. Inquire
then, Job, amid the afflictions of your fate,
whence cometh all this shattering Providence?
Man's poverty is humbling. Its heavy ore
is iron, and the Worm is but a parasite
of fraudulent deceit – O insolence!
Smooth traitor, with a kiss... *Iago, Esquire!*

La condition humaine – our common plight.
We dig these complex and inventive pits
to bury enemies, neighbors (ourselves, in spite).
And so when Sheba tested Solomon, his wits
gave way... he was espoused to *Sophia;*
yet Sheba showed him more (all through the night).
Follow the shadow of a dove, Jonah, that flits
beyond your gutted lamp... toward daylight.

10.4.24

FAMILIAR HOME

The fevered reds and orange of the autumn trees –
a circle of fire, ringing winter's zero to come.
On our Minnesota flag (mine and Sophie's),
a little green pine stretches up to azure dome,
planted in a small half-moon of purple shade.
It's dark out, now. The spooky travesties
of haunted Halloween already twitch the fiefdom.
All ghosts on their lonely farms come back, milord.
All cricket sadness of the prairie earth... is yours.

A tiny gnat flits, after the sudden sundown,
over the kitchen lampshade. We all seek warmth
and light. Each hearth-flame is your own
heart-furnace – Osip's *domestic hellenism.*
The teleology of fire, our own familiar home.
Empedocles himself – Etna his crown
of ash – witnessed the roaring *charism*
(so windy!) of her rosy-fingered kingdom –
whose shade is violet... whose banner's known.

My charming fantasies, Sophie... are what they are.
They say the problem of the mind is "quality".
Grace and Truth (that is, AMOR)
are tested on the anvil of reality.
Your armorer is like the summer sun :
she burns all night, above the Finland air
and hammers out her golden grail of charity.
Vain little man came, that we all be one –
unknown soldier, shaggy ink-cap. Star.

10.5.24

MY PLUMB-LINE

October darkness falls too soon.
I cannot work in my gazebo now
(too cold, too dark). My avocado moon
swims, like an ancient wedding vow
sealed beneath Earth's muddy green garden.
Love's word is humble. Simple is her tune.
Anonymous shepherd's glance (her quizzical brow).
The *Chakarshambeh Suri* celebration
baptizes (with fire) Earth's meek pontoon.

Imagine a Viking burial ship, set aflame
and pushed away from shore. Or Noah's Ark,
grounded on Ararat – a whole new frame
for this mournful globe. Twain, mark :
my plumb-line drops to the bottom of the sea.
Young Peter the Great played a royal game
at Amsterdam (in camouflage, just for a lark);
yet the guileful heart is more disguised than he –
coiled in the adamant of one jay-haunted Name.

A poem is a sort of scything sigh.
What weighs upon my heart I cannot say :
a kind of cankered anchor? Look to the sky,
Hamlet, Kierkegaard … the sun's up there today,
as every day – burning with an active charity.
Some jovial and versatile *Ahilyabai*
– or Everywoman, Everyman – who shines that way
because the *Son of Man* is like the sun – see?
See? Light shines in the darkness. (*Hai*.)

10.6.24

SWIM WITH ME

My quiet cricket, like a typewriter sonata
softly mimes the August grandeur of cicadas,
as the autumn sun tilts her planet-piñata
like some sea-coracle, heeled by the breeze
'til her deep keel resists, and rights the ship –
with a b-flat drone below all our antennae
that murmurs down the woody spine... Athena's
fire-light, sparking like a serpent-whip.
You know the tale, I think (dry *Argonautica*).

We dust the universe with our mythologies.
The heavy machinery of too much knowledge
tempts us merely to de-familiarize –
Prometheus still shackled along that ledge;
thus we miss the tiny cricket-lamp of *soul*.
Pale moon-pearl, hid from prying eyes
beneath an avocado's dark green sedge,
you mirror one far point of fire – unroll
(through your mudlands) integral Paradise.

O moon, you float in absolute silence
there at the matrix of each trickster heart.
O heart, a-tremble in grey fur of sentience
(passionate, patient, bearing all hurt...)
you quicken to the signal of that last cricket –
win my wine, my sun, my winsome benevolence...
like a chelys *ukelele, play your turtledove part;*
like a kayak in a coracle, a naval mirror in my locket,
swim with me, Jonah – *I am LOVE's intelligence.*

10.7.24

LET LOVE INCREASE

The crescent moon, so warm and close tonight
over the maple sentinels along the street;
bright packet-boat, upon your lonely flight
flashing a message only morning will complete.
Your ancient rightness is so close at hand.
Truth belongs to little ones : their trusting light!
Primordial wisdom was... simple and sweet!
So human gemstones issue one command :
rise, blossom, burning rose – your heart!

When immortal spirit molted into flesh
the moon became an avocado in the Earth.
Her camouflage (so green, anonymous)
seeded the planet with an equal worth –
all things grew choral in that submarine.
What we sensed in the beginning, sprang afresh...
again! A goodness harbored there, from birth!
Just so the young boy shakes his tambourine –
just so the dancer lofts her salty wish!

Now the fires rage, and burning will not cease,
it seems. Yet you feel the good fire... the bonfire.
Like a drifting leaf, like a floating *feuille*, you are –
would that you knew the things that make for peace.
So close to the center of this conflagration...
my blind, my troubled soul yearns for release.
Then my immurèd Moon murmurs : *inquire,*
my son. I am your Advocate – your close relation.
So may my guard go down. Let love increase.

10.8.24

TACONITE EMPIRE

October pumpkin man forsakes his gazebo
for the memory-basement (family archives).
Granddad's blueprint, unbuilt long ago –
his cabin by Two Island. The long knives
of the Taconite Empire – *by eminent domain* –
stole it away from Lake Superior
and Ravlin family. Thus Babel strives
to raise a tower, on the rocks of Everyman :
sharp rocks of Mammon's weal, to commons woe.

The basement's full of many maps, of wilderness.
And my own scrawl's only a place-keeper
for dew-drawn meadows – old man's absence.
Parmenides, likewise, scented the reaper...
thus your nine blistering rings, O Goddess!
To play the cosmic chunky-ball of Nicolas
you must be touched by charismatic fire.
VENI, mandorla... *UNIONEQUALITY*! with *CARITAS*!
Drink deep from Noah's wine, Jason – Odysseus!

The gift of life, down in my scholar's tomb.
O pedant Poe, trickster librarian –
whose words like dust yearn for that little room
where such rude goodness comes to life again...
that rosy-fingered, equable morning
borne out of Earth's unfathomable womb.
And this, my song, only a faulty sign –
lofted by grey wings of turtledove (humming).
Moon-haunts of pumpkin man (*Halloween*, I presume).

10.10.24

THE GOLD RING

It was good to walk paths of Lebanon Hills today.
Poplars, oaks, maples lifted their warm fire
in unison, up to the pale blue sky.
Meantime, their namesake is consumed by war.
The will of God is peace – harvest of equity.
Yet men forego that path, taking another way.
Dominion of brute force... pure faithless ire.
Turn back, these wise trees whisper (quietly).
Le feu de joie is HEARTH-FIRE : *c'est la clé.*

Sometimes we must sink to the volcanic floor
to be lifted up. I spent a sweaty morning
underground, in my mother's cold pottery lair –
sifting like a sullen Poe, on mission forlorn
through mountainous inkwell archives of my past.
Until... out of that labyrinth of *nevermore*
her tiny, holiday *shalom*-bird came gliding...
from what bright vortex all her clay was cast!
– spun with twirling *agape* to the world's door.

My mother's heart forged many deeds of love –
my mother's art birthed tumbling fleets of glee
for many children (young and old). It was the dove,
Jonah, nestled in your name – your Jubilee.
Meek feathers, for a human happiness;
an arc-light, slanting down from far above
that tempers wrath with sapient humility –
so rose the gold ring that makes the iron move.

10.12.24

LIGHT RAINBOW

A west wind riffles through October leaves
and a whiff of cold earmarks the difference
between mind and body. A raven weaves
the destiny of souls. *The rest is silence,*
per Prince Hamlet (and Cautantowwit).
Gather round the fire; bring in the sheaves;
time has come to harvest labor – dance,
Grace! Soon winter puts an end to it. Yet
you shall smile (whose cricket-heart still grieves).

Elijah, Empedocles – both miracle-workers –
both children once, helping feed the hearth.
That evening sun is evening the Earth;
fire circles round the circle round the fire,
Empedocles, Elias. Trees flame in the woods
with a good strife, not an evil one, *señor;*
the good man celebrates her mother-worth
at his long table, in the poorest neighborhoods.
Moon molts to sun (light monarch, everywhere).

Noah lay naked and drunk outside his gazebo,
dreaming of the Ark. Firewater surged like wind
all through his burning bowels. He was *Jonah,*
buried in the whale… and then the whale let go.
Got up, walked – down into Nineveh.
Shouted – *the word is* MELK, *people! You've sinned –
turn back to* MELK! *And end your long sorrow.*
So Noah stumbled – flipped his ukelele…
overhead a monarch floated (light rainbow).

10.13.24

53

CANDLE'S BOON

Before the winter's iron, woods turn to bronze.
Zeal for my Mother's barge consumeth me
when I behold my haunted Myrmidons
fall upon themselves (with tempered enmity).
Rose from the land of Ire – fell for Achilles…
yarrow's yellow gold heals not their wounds.
Her avocado's green. *È vero, si?*
Verona earth turns emerald (Veronese)
when MELK and Henry J. join *shalom* hands.

You note the puzzle in my pregnant speech.
The *Unknown Soldier* braves an unknown strife.
Buried in grass… *once more unto the breach,*
my friend… your shaggy ink-cap shield's my life!
Grows of itself, like every blessèd thing –
no force, no fear, no whitening bleach
restrains a rose husbandman from his black wife.
See there, where *Jonah Rainbow-Neck* takes wing!
(*Iris is avocado green, softened by peach.*)

We labor in the earth to find your moon –
your barge, my advocate. Tender you glide
above the autumn fires, our sad cocoon
of blind and troubled hibernation; wide
spreads the silver compass of your AGAPE
– your pity for Man's foolishness (undone).
They know not what they do. Your green kid,
pale Jonah, climbs from the avocado's bay –
walks back to Nineveh. Lights candle's boon.

10.14.24

SPRIGHTLY PHALAROPE

These clouds are silver-grey, overcast on blue.
The scattering leaves, in our continual drought
are brown and dry – lonesome from leaving you,
tall tree. I want to find thee out,
autumnal *Providence*. I want to reach
up through that leafy maze of long ago
into your fiery gold of maple-heart –
tasting the syrup that you came to teach.
A parable : somehow happy, somehow true.

Our planet revolves to face the *Day of the Dead*.
For centuries, the ghost in the machine
withdrew. Material measures took the lead.
And yet, toward the incalculable unseen
the human mind inexorably turned –
like aging intellect, in old gray head.
Good night, Irene, good night, Irene...
sweet clay of Aristotle (Grecian, urned)...
Be still! 'Tis haunted (*life's high meed*).

The knots in this wooden heart of mine, I hope
still swell, slightly, with sap. Because the mind
alone cannot find you out, Riddle. Nope.
The mind – from animal to angel – is unkind
or kind, somehow. Refined upon its wheel
of autumn fire – a sprightly phalarope –
the heart swims deeper than the mind has mined.
Like Wisdom, whispering under the keel
and up your spine... (so blind men grope).

10.19.24

PAPYRUS RUSTLING

These trees are burning, with a playful fire.
An autumn fire, not of our making.
One with the planet's vernal curvature
that leafs to ashes (late November raking).
The maples' bronze and gold are integral :
bold as the black-eyed Susans' flower
brightens the field – summer not forsaking.
Their sunny choir sings, *all shall be well*
though petals fall, and yellow-gold expire.

There's meager comfort in such natural signs,
for hearts full-shattered on the wheel of woe.
For minds grown gloomy, as their day declines –
as dear ones disappear (we watch them go).
Truth burns, Empedocles... in your volcano!
That thin gold leaf, troved in Hipponian mines
still glimmers, *in memoriam*... Psyche, Io!
Día de Muertos... – Again, Señora Gregorio!
My body is... all-human (bread and wine).

We are the spume... salt excess of the universe.
The spray... that, out of one bright cubicle
floats to a playful crown... (none can rehearse).
Yes! Out of one lightweight deerskin coracle
your flower of creation blooms... one *Rose*.
Reverberating through her turtleshell cosmos,
as we curve too, into your smiling spectacle...
Leave your papyrus rustling, kid. Come, nurse.

10.20.24

ACORN CROWNS

Indian Summer... in October (not
November). Henry the mute blindfolded seer
remains sequestered in his 8-fold hut
of ancient cedar. Wicked by the grease of pure
greed, unaccountable power, neglected Earth
succumbs to dry fever – charcoaled by rot.
It's not what anybody wants to hear.
Great crowds are fizzing with a funded mirth
(anything to tip the lottery of human lot).

Blind Milton pours out what weighs upon his heart,
his tongue mingling old fables with wisdom,
intuiting some rightness at the start
(his *Providence*). All oracles are dumb
as well as blind : merely a dove croons
through his drab and blurry dawn. *Depart,*
my soul, into your silver-grey freedom!
Wide sea of wracking gulls, of lonesome loons...
– so, among the stars (like fireflies) we float.

Somehow we are at home in this cosmos.
Your constancy, your equanimity –
dependable and imperturbable resource...
soul-source; like harbored *Liberty,*
stony, salty. Like Roger in Rhode Island,
or Blackstone up on Beacon Hill, our *nostos*
is that fiery hearth of rightness : *charity*!
Telos of every journey – planned, unplanned;
gold shadow, glinting in rough oak-tree boughs.

Now we become familiar with lost ghosts
again, and the ghost of loss (they are the same).
Halloween – a gathering of hosts
we never thanked enough. *I'll take the blame,*
cries Pumpkin Man. Just then his eyes light up :
and far beyond, off Black Sea coasts
a St.-John's-fire shows on the topmast... *Lamb*
of God, be with us now! Descend... to sup!
Pray for us sailors – teach us your *Paternost*!

So the sea draws us out, and the land draws us back.
Recall old Shaidlock Negus, family man,
shepherd and orchardist – guiding his flock
from Pennsylvania, out to Iowa (green
meadow oceans)... to Springdale Meeting House.
And as war loomed, for North and South, Shaidlock
and Quaker friends gave refuge to John Brown –
despite their absolute disdain for violence.
So turtledoves are grey... not white nor black.

We travel out at night, under the stars,
and learn to be at home, at sea. The soul
is something constant and mysterious –
knotted with anchor cable to the Eternal;
yet that rope runs through the center of the Earth.
Somehow the heart bears all this weight and mass –
and there emerges her enigma, like the bole
that swells from one great oak of death and birth.
Mother of acorn crowns... and the end of wars.

10.22.24

SPINE TINGLES

A cold wind from the north – dry foretaste of November.
We have weathered these seasons many times before.
Young Lexi, my neighbor, is groaning next door –
birth-pangs. May she be well; may her child be limber.
Night is dark and clear… air washes the cedars
as by a wind from the sea. And I remember
Rhode Island – wild roses on the shore,
wise words of brave Roger : that zeal JOY inspires.
In AGAPE's galactic hearth, each soul's a filial ember.

I would give you my *summa* before winter comes.
Have read some philosophers – Parmenides,
Empedocles… cogent contemporary Nagel,
Robinson – yet wild, remote Berkeley remains
a star. Staring out toward the sea
from solitary Newport cliff, perhaps he hums
some luminous and melancholy Irish reel.
Music… sweet ineffability.
Her Lapp-wave pleads : *taste my mead, fishcrumbs.*

Words are but words; songs are but jingles.
Multifarious human deeds mean more,
pierce deeper to the core, of singular things.
Meek soldiers of the unknown went before.
Your fathers, mothers, to the sundown stream
where hurricane tears off the shingles –
earthquake shakes the Quakers to the floor.
We are – we share – the filiations of one Dream :
Ark, *Argo*, sweeping home… (spine tingles).

10.22.24

THE TURTLEDOVE

Henry lingers, overripe, in his gazebo, now
like yearning, palpitating Oblomov,
despite the chill of late October. How
dry it is, how dry! Twigs with the bloom off
crackle underfoot. Great looming oaks
are desiccated too, and suffering. We know
it all, without knowing : the national stove
is baking its dead branches. We old folks
are passing away. Better head back to Glasgow,

Mary Gold Galloway Bryce ("May")! Too late
to change again – too late to move.
This dryness rattles like a skeletal Fate,
stretching her bony hand to the candy trove
at Halloween. So let it rain – rain!
The chess set in our political attic (*checkmate!*)
plays itself : red, blue... liberal, conservative...
dollars change hands... graft trundles back again.
Return, *gae* Edinburgh? – *Your ticket's out of date.*

Your great-aunt May became a staunch American,
Henry. Interred in Lakewood Cemetery
beneath gaunt, regal and brooding oaks. Gone
to ground – her body, anyway. Soul? Not for me
to know (or say). Yet... at the end of May...
a breeze, a breath... of green Resurrection.
Uncanny! Like a Selkie out of Sligo (aye)
a prophet strokes her coracle – to Restoration Day!
We'll sail together, gal... across wide OKEAN!

Oblomov, wobbly Noah, mumbles in his cups.
There are no miracles in Science (though
you may wonder); superstition corrupts
the little mind there is – and *ye shall know
the Truth; the Truth shall set you free.* See?
– Not so easily. Jesus, at the wedding nups,
turns water into wine... how so, Horatio?
We keep one another for eternity,
brother : Love is the ratio that sums us up.

So love is rational – to a surreal extent!
Reason of reason's like the Ghost of ghosts –
she comes at midnight into Noah's tent,
shows him the plan for her canoe... it floats!
As *Raven* and the *Dove*, who glide together
over the surface of a sphere... a parallax, bent
(relaxed) along the border of a duplex coast –
like *Eire* in Ireland – with shamrock tether!
May every Galloway swim with such true intent!

The wind in my scribble-hut grows inexorably colder,
scribbles Henry. It's Halloween – the Fiend
is at the door. America just gets older,
not more just. Yet there's a gold ring, my friend :
a wedding band, inscribed : ÉGALITÉ.
Not equal in status, looks... equal in honor.
Honor, like light, drifts down from far beyond
our time, our space – borne from eternity
on pinions of grace... the *Turtledove*. Enfold her.

10.23.24

TO JOHN BERRYMAN

It rained last night, at last – a blessing, John.
Early in the morning, on your birthday.
Rained across Tower Hill – went brimming down
the copper-green of the Witch's Hat – away
down Arthur Avenue… past your last hideout.
The oaks are happy; all the trees in town
breathe easier, grow young and green, today.
You sleep across the river still, old goat –
in Resurrection Cemetery. How be born again?

You were a Catholic man of faith (for better
or worse); my gr-great-Granddad and his father
(from Dublin) were Baptists, to the letter –
preachers, pioneers. Abolitionists, for sure.
Yet how shall man or woman be born again?
(enquires old Arimathea). Heart is the center
of human affections : justice the signature
for each affectionate deed. The dignity of Man
shines from such loving works (heart of the matter).

The green heart of the Earth shall be reborn
like a child's adoration for the sunrise,
out of doors. Gold glinting on the corn –
joy anchored in heart's plummet (to the skies).
Plunge your brow into the river, child –
the *Ocean River* (rainbow over every barn).
The *Ark*, the *Argo*… through *Aurora Borealis*
pioneer your Way. The path is wild,
and snarled, and true – Polaris knots the yarn,

*

and Giuliana threads the loom. Raven,
Ravenna's near. Your *Henry*, Berryman,
has a new name : she's born again.
Rhodri. Out of Rhode Island, then?
From Wales, originally. Bright Henry V
of Agincourt – of Gaunt, silvery gold mine –
young Jack, asleep in Dallas (milky, slain)…
our hosts are whorled into five-fathom depth.
Arise, *Ariel* – sail again, *Rhodri* (wheelsman)!

So the heart murmurs. Not *against* the mind, exactly :
contrapuntal. The mind, Parmenides,
is set upon the truth… like a block of снег,
Yuki. Many a cat is frozen in those lees,
Pushkin – many a Zen stone, sanded in Kyoto.
This mumbling dove – who wanders on your sea,
Jonah… she bears an olive (avocado's
moon). Love's bond, beyond what mind can know.
Her gravity lifts graves – to monarch's ecstasy.

You wonder at my muttering! No doubt –
it stands to reason. We have walked through rain
o'er Tower Hill… have stood upon redoubt
at Glastonbury. Heart will rise, and reign again,
AGAPE triumph over tyranny :
because the soul of Man is like Achilles (stout,
yet vulnerable). The heart is like Ismene :
clambers from the dead , in Thessaly –
keen wisdom's keel. She tells us what it's all about.

10.25.24

III

The Grail

RHODY, RHODRI

Halloween. Man, like hollowed-out pumpkin
with toothy grin, suddenly becomes,
for a while, all candlelight. When children
arrive at the door (aglow themselves) in costumes
whimsical and winsome... and Night looks on
in the background, quiet and profound (like
                                        Raven).
While further out, *Coulombe* is doing her sums :
souls form a Union (human-&-divine).
It is *All-Hallows* after all, munchkin.

A breezy sketch, black ink on white.
My mother *fecit*, 60 years ago.
Kid, bent over delicate sandcastle (quite
intent). A ziggurat, with tiny flag, just so –
Old Glory. Careless waves receive the shore
behind him... and I'm suddenly rapt in spirit
back to Goosewing (in Rhode Island). O
my oneiric *Ocean State*... realm of *Nevermore*
and evermore. Roger's *Eternity* (Cautantowwit).

Consciousness we cannot quantify;
character we cannot paraphrase;
heart we cannot plumb. The child's eye
sees, however : *and for all my days*
Lord Father-Mother, I will follow you.
Philia lofts us, like an eagle, to the sky –
while down below, Roger's bright *compagnevole*
braves all that spite and callousness can do.
He sets his seal on *Providence* (Rhody, Rhodri).
                                        10.31.24

TWISTED KNOT

The readiness is all. *The hour comes,*
Horatio – the KAIROS. *My spirit*
hovers, slightly silvered by my arms...
this autumn chill is haunted. Look to it.
Guy Fawkes... bonfires and skyrockets,
laughter of crowds. And to the throb of drums
the traitor's body – disemboweled, split
among four corners of the kingdom – frets
only the conscience of Judge Coke... (condemns).

Election Day. The traitor, *redivivus*,
golden-orange, breathing fire, emerges
from Hecate's diamond basement (Hades)...
wearing Empedocles' bronze shoe. Jesus!
No one could have predicted this. *Amen,*
howls each mesmerized hurt soul... *He's us!*
Meanwhile... Roger, Coke's fiery lamb... sighs.
These trials of conscience burden suffering MAN!
he shouts : *Only soft-hearted* JONAH *can restore us.*

War's end is *District of Columbia.*
Or Narragansett Bay. I recall that photo
of young JFK, lounging barefoot and carefree,
reading his book aboard a sloop (you know
the one). That Pentecostal dove floats down...
touching the circle (on his own birthday)
with fire. *I learn by going where I have to go.*
Wheat's in the barn : feeding both sheep and goats.
Come back, America. Your twisted knot untie.

11.4.24

SEA-ROSE BAND

In a dark time, the eye begins to see

The misty calm across the river today
belies the sudden fall of winter's dark.
Down through 9 infernal circles, Dante
somersaults… right to the nadir's murk.
Here in America, we hoist a flag
turned *black green orange*. It is the mark
of Antichrist – flipped round, vice-versa.
Sheba, your advocate, turned cruel hag –
Solomon, in Petersburg, *complètement gelé*.

The Idol puffs his cheeks. Even his odor
mars the calm lake-surface of the stream.
His venom stings both sheep, who adore
and panting wolves, ravenous for more (dream
of Macbeth, polishing his burning wood
like brass). It is the Emperor – his hour;
his silver sperm is nothing like ice cream.
No golden bough anneals his frigid brood –
each dead heart's welded to one arctic shore.

That boy, molding his ziggurat of sand
on Narragansett Beach, sets a tiny *Old Glory*
at the apex. O thy crumbling reprimand
of Law – *Old Ironsides*! Say… can you see?
Sheba, my *Avocado*… rescue me
and mine! Sheep scatter across the island :
shepherds of Mammon be their destiny!
Still… hearts harbor justice (with a sea-rose band).

11.6.24

THE BEES BEGIN

If you walk the narrow arc of the universe
between heaven and earth, as Dante did
along that curve between two hyperspheres
like a Venn diagram, or the back of a katydid –
just as Elijah, in his flaming chariot,
or Parmenides, dragged by four horses
of the Sun Goddess... you'll see what has been hid
from sun-blind vision, since humanity was not :
the curving eyebrows of our fleet cosmos.

Elijah and Parmenides were both stern-men.
Both very stern : they knew how far below
they were from what's above, beyond their ken.
They glimpse her lucent eye upon the prow
like far-off twinkling, as in a mirror –
across vast space... bent back again
without an edge : basking, replete, somehow
(as summer meadows burgeon into flower). So
her glance brightens their minds' eye, like a sign.

Angelic vision in a mortal frame
possessed rapt Dante, and these other two;
what threw them for a loop at first, became
like arrows fitted to a bow of yew
sharp measures of a true bull's-eye.
Ethereal buoyancy, too sweet to name...
when love's eye lingers, in the heart of you.
And suddenly there's no more dying! *Cry
no more*... Beatrice's taken aim.

How walk on earth then, in this Ark of arcs?
Straight ahead, neither to right nor left
the curve will lead you where disaster lurks –
lift up your willow rod, tracing the weft
crosswise – against the drag of gravity –
up to the purling of a spiral spring. Marks
(on a rock there) map the way – a rainbow shift
through water-drops… mirage to reality;
here's where your bobbing coracle embarks.

Heartbeats measure the immeasurable soul
and wisdom (high *Sophia*, deep *Athena*)
shores the wooden ribs, spine of the keel
with sap – with sapience. Remember now
your mother, and your father… *agape*, and *philia*;
bear with such hardships of your trial
and reckon all your joys – rising to awe.
Let goodness keep you jovial (*selah*) :
around your boat currents of *Ocean River* flow.

And when that distempered bull from the sea
                                               arrives
to bore at the foundations of your house,
be not dismayed – always good labor strives
to build, not to destroy. The earth's your spouse;
you shall fulfill the mutual promise of your vow.
So keep your covenant together. Like Argives'
galley-in-a-bottle, she's a replica of COSMOS –
keep sailing. Her smiling eye is on the prow.
From EQUALITY (her rose evening) JUSTICE
                                                derives.

Look neither right nor left, Solomon, Solon.
The cash cow of the State is not for sale
though she be soft-hearted, benevolent (*amen*);
rapacious wolves, beneath sign of the Bull
be not your governors, but rampant thieves.
Their judge is *Unknown Soldier* – Everywoman,
Everyman – a U.S. Grant against Leeward Rebel.
The people drift away, like windblown leaves...
yet justice is their last criterion.

The Bull is bold as brass – yet fraudulent.
It's his Achilles heel (yarrow won't heal).
Offers himself, like Antichrist, as heaven-sent...
sure! I smell that golden toilet bowl... unreal.
Money will assuage neither left nor right
nor will it appease these mobs, grown virulent.
They do not represent the people... *commonweal*,
and I could beat my bully drum on this, all night.
Make America grieve again : that's what he meant.

Revenge, the stuff of tragedy, is dumb.
Resentment, like a canker-sore, is blind.
I do not mean to mock those who are numb –
Jesus! You sure know how to put us in a bind.
Poe glares back, from his locked room (poetry).
Antarctica... iceberg he could not plumb.
Nor can we (Satan is wheedling, just behind).
Suddenly this fog of mirages lifts... behold, *Psyche*.
The mirror brims with light; the bees begin to
                                        hum.

11.7.24

CLOUD-BED

The Emperor dragged his spear along the ground
trailing a phantom angel, as he paced along
tracing his New Rome, marking the bound.
Projecting there, on foot and by furlong
something invisible as that angel's wings –
a new sacred graveyard (human ant-mound).
Already rural folk registered a strong
antipathy : the iron spear-point stings :
and yet those shackled yokels make no sound

that togas in the Forum might propound.
These men are oxen, yoked to heavy labor!
Their families, figments of the grim surround –
hoarse cries, hard lifting... beggar-neighbor!
Our flitting guile shall work a short-cut – sing
Arms and the Man, O noble Homer... clown
a little, even – splendid banquet, in the manor!
Let me show you round the royal Angel Wing –
stylish, sophisticated... plus, profound!

The silent Emperor walks straight ahead.
Stares down into the dirt – attempts to catch
the slightest flicker of that angel's tread.
A farmer on the sidelines strikes a match,
lights a primitive cigarette (*Constantine's
Delight*). We are but mirrors, someone said.
The King, the slave – both wear eye-patch;
only a healer can repair this scene.
Blind eyes lift up... behold a city on cloud-bed.

11.8.24

THE DAUPHIN

Rhodri was but a boy – just a pip of a lad.
Servant to jolly Roger, the rudder-man,
who judged the kid's vision not half-bad
(a pilot's help). Meanwhile, the grim Captain,
up at the prow, flanked by his decked-out minions,
threatened with hellfire any salt gone mad.
Rhodri trembled with fear and consternation –
his angry eye, his glittering pinions
threatened the knout of God to all on board.

His inscrutable will was like a math puzzle
too hard for unschooled Rhodri. How could it be
that a Spirit swift as light, whose galactic dazzle
dwarfed Ocean itself, could be like me? *Like* me?
His head (unable to grasp the ungraspable)
leant against the mast. *Look to the crow's eyrie,*
a voice whispered. High up, winds wrestled
with cloud, with sail... Behold, a Round Table!
St.-Elmo's Fire – a sparkling shamrock whorl!
                              *

Sunlight's muted as a silver trumpet now.
November limps along, toward Veteran's Day.
I ponder fabulous Rhodri – knit my brow...
and shrug. No match will spark what I portray.
I lack the words for that damned *Jonah*-boat,
filled with fallible hearts – no grace will endow.
In Paris, eight iron bells ring out. A roundelay
of joy... to celebrate that stone dovecôte
restored, at last : her ancient shoulders, shining
                                        brow.

The cigarette that set those spires ablaze
played emissary for our feeble state,
in general. Yet good will shall amaze :
hearts' will, springing to liberate
our melancholy selves, with *commonweal*.
Good labor, wrecks restore : the dead shall raise.
In-woven minds and hearts bring forth *spirit* –
their byzantine enameled tapestry is real.
So beauty lifts the mind... where *rightness* plays.

*

When I remember your green wheel, ripe avocado,
fleur-de-lys... my contradictions fuse
and morph into some lighter, aerial *Mikado*.
Gentle *coulombe*, your penetrating Muse
(my Beatrice) charms the Mind to reconcile
with Heart, and Will with all that souls can do :
until the universe becomes a cruise
away from slavery – *liberty* for you, my chile!
Rhodri knows, now... that is Love's table-menu.

Philosophers and scientists will show
they're having second thoughts about this, too.
We wander disenchanted, here below –
forget what Nicolas of Cusa knew
he didn't know... but felt. O cheerful heart,
soft Advocate... a-brim with your glow
that arcs down, like a dolphin – lifts anew;
sealed on my brow, as she was, from the start –
divine bird, child of God... dusted with snow.

11.10.24

RED-PLUM CALF

after Osip Mandelstam

At Arlington, the flags wave farewell,
and muted silver taps like a woodpecker
while drones and helicopters spin their spell.
Vainamonen's at his forge, the ironmonger –
shaping his *Sampo* like a long canoe,
hoping to Finn it up from his arctic Hell.
Hoisting his silver shield – that bold maker,
that vain little man, that Smith, that me and you.
They buried Unknown Soldier in a turtle shell.

Under a sprinkling snow at Spring Lake Park
we found a shaggy ink-cap... Shakespeare's cap.
Domed and bronze as Achaean helmet – marked
with a gash across the crown. And through a gap
in the galaxies, light poured down fire...
melting Smith's features to a *Jonah*-scrap
(curving feather, broken wing). Too dark!
Vainamonen, mired in mud, crawled to the pyre –
black hole, nailed coffin-cosmos. Funeral bark.

Men's admonitions raise a bitter laugh.
He's Vainamonen – hero – unknown soldier!
Dragging himself across his own epitaph
toward dawn, his arms grow moldier –
mind grows colder – heart grows warmer!
Through fetid caves THOU *leadest me... thy staff*
doth comfort me... mother, father, sister, brother!
Thy silver-grey JONAH – no one can harm her.
Rays in clouds surround him... like a red-plum
                                        calf.

11.11.24

76

MY SNOWFLAKES

Blackbird singing in the dead of night…

My blackbird sings out of the limbs of autumn.
Bare in the bear-wind, shivering toward sleep.
The wind blows cool; where it comes from
no one knows. Some frosted *loch*, some keep
high in the mountains of the sky… cloud-castle.
All the meek oven-birds have scurried home
as best they can… yet the abyss is deep.
Fear stalks them, through the cindery stubble;
music of the lightning-whip, the thunder-drum.

The heart is a Smith, hammering upon his forge.
He melts the harsh fire in the falling leaves
into a fiercer, molten hearth – his dirge
into a steely shield. His family bereaves
in vain : he's Vainamonen! Will climb back
from arctic *Ocean's* phosphorescent gorge,
as hearts take heart within funereal graves;
as sparks, flung from galactic *Way-Way-Back*,
warm nests in Ithaca, or Bethlehem (light-surge)

to shout across rooftops : *Let* LOVE *increase!*
Her one-point star – immaterial, remote –
here welded to your heart – is Truth, is Peace!
Soul unto spirit hewn, each dusty mote –
each *Unknown Soldier* – flashes her semaphore
of Joy – O ecstasy of heart's release!
Courage, *Everyhuman* – *Man-o'War* is stout!
I come to cast fire upon the Earth once more,
he roars – and laughs! *So may my snowflakes never*
cease!

11.13.24

THE GRAIL

Today, in 332 B.C., great Alexander
was crowned Pharaoh of Egypt. Also, today
is my Alex's birthday. Moreover,
in 1920, the Finns began to play
Pesäpollo : *nest-ball*, or "Finnish baseball"
(Vainamonen would have certainly won). Later,
in 1960, "Ted" Maiman patented the ruby
laser – the same day Ruby Bridges walked tall
into that all-white school. Courageous pioneer!

Hard to breathe sometimes, under the smoky glass
of this echoing railroad station. Trains clank,
winds roar every way – who hears you now,
                                 Aonides?
For moral freedom... whom have I to thank?
Freedom of conscience : *basis of Soul Liberty*,
Roger proclaimed. There, with his exile's pass
and robe of Canonicus...while angels, rank on rank
bestowed their *seraph*-seal upon humanity – *crown
of creation* (God's own laddie, God's own lass).

Our life's a complex game of nest-ball, Nicolas
of Cusa thought. Opinions matter, somewhat –
but not so much as deeds of love, of strife. Grass,
bending in the wind, we are : yet there's a boat
that knits us all together to its curving keel.
A stone boat – fallen from the sky, perhaps –
an emerald advocate, with ruby heart –
a rose-clay cup we sail, with sea-rose wheel –
The Grail. And little Rhodri turns the windlass.
                                 11.14.24

CRYSTAL CAVES

The last of the golden leaves come falling now.
O season of loneliness and memory!
I turn to Osip's, Paul Celan's, know-how :
LOGOS is message-in-a-bottle, meant for me.
Ross Russell, of the Corsewall Lighthouse, knows
– that letter in a jar, stowed 132 years ago
in a dead man's wall, was writ *to thee* – to thee
only! Row as we might, the tide still flows...
leaves fall...the lighthouse rides upon Time's brow.

I was lost beneath a marble Whisper Dome.
The enigmatic fresco on the ceiling,
whorled in clouds of Judgement Day to come
like a grim tornado, held me – dizzy, reeling –
'til a soft murmur rippled from the other side.
Held me upright : in balance again. Home.
As at the center of some luminous ring
infinitely high and deep (and galaxies wide)...
a moon at avocado's heart : a human Rome.
                              *

Ted Olson died : famous conservative lawyer.
I heard him interviewed, on NPR.
He spoke of clashing opinions (Tom Sawyer,
Huck Finn... Left, Right) – how they are
divisive, yet needn't be. *All due respect*.
With tolerance – equable toward one another –
all things are possible. A peacemaker
he was (*blessèd are they*). Behold this prospect :
O Happy Day, people! No fear, bias... no special
                                        favor.

Recall that soul, exiled for tolerance
at the beginning of these querulous States.
Tossed outright into winter's snowy silence –
saved by kind Canonicus, Cautantowwit.
This was a man who carried his own compass
into the wilderness, and learned to dance :
dance *1-3-2*. A Narragansett waltz
of fellowship, beneath one far Polaris –
one *triste tendresse*, below that light's entrance.

*

So the dry leaf swims down to her green grave.
The snow will drift across Rhode Island
before long. Memories, in one wave
scar their shells... Time cannot mend.
My soul's a pilgrim, in a waist-deep marsh;
the shore's just over there – you must be brave!
Yet heroism is no magic wand.
Heart's recompense for one's own sin is harsh;
just one grey whisper-bird may grief relieve.

*

Outside, the world's awash in brooding fire.
Empedocles, beneath his own volcano
left a bronze shoe for Hecate – ensign of ire.
Strife and corruption and untruth we know,
yet reckon not the cost of our own wrath.
It is the sum of each blind, vain desire,
poured on our heads like Caribbean guano :
hatred in Haiti – poverty in Bath!
Billionaire demons, singing in a choir...

Parmenides, roped by horses of the sun
warned of illusion in the realm of Man.
Truth is a motionless, silent block of *One*
– cold as burning ice – remotely taciturn...
(such attributes themselves *subject to change*).
What draws me to him, though, is like heartburn :
the pain of LOVE, his unmistakable passion.
Love calls him, to come home – *home on the range!*
Hoofbeats thunder... (Aphrodite's acumen).

*

Eros is blind. The poet's blind as well.
Justice is blind... the measure of the real
is chance, is fate – disinterested swell,
subsiding on the shore. Our *commonweal*,
shifty and changeable... life's rugged school.
Follow your inclinations straight to Hell;
or hearken to that dove, whose song you feel.
All flesh on Earth obeys one granite rule –
Love others as yourself (hear the round bronze bell).

My syllables rise and fall across the waves
like autumn leaves, gilded by the cold.
Toward love the body churns – the mind slaves;
Eros gets rusty, as the flesh grows old.
Yet light as aspen leaf is charity!
The heart knows this, before the mind believes.
Heart sparks the will – heart breaks the mold.
And at its rosy wheel, a Galilean Rhodri
leads the way... steers toward deep Crystal Caves.

11.17.24

COMPASS ROSE

To be a good Greek is all my study now.
I listened for your throaty song, Psyche-
Hermione... and Simone showed me how
(wily, wisely). You're beautiful to me.
Psyche, the ship that sank with pure *La Paix*
was sundered by a raging bull-sow
whale – who also thumped *Statue of Liberty*.
He knows nothing of *Life* – nor *Truth*, nor *Way*.
LOVE mediates all harmony – not that grim brow!

You must be perfect, little children, lambs.
What does this mean? Study geometry,
and see! The 3rd between 2 mean iambs
conjoins the *Alma Trimeter* of poetry :
thus hymns of Apollonios of Rhodes
leap from a spring whence perfect beauty streams.
Open your heart... taste original joy!
Soul freedom is that gold no rust corrodes –
a-gleam in Hestia's cosmic flame (the great I AM).

Down chill November streets of Providence
weak Edgar Poe beseeched poor Helen Whitman :
Marry me, I beg you! – met with silence.
It was too late. Yet, overhead, Orion
sailed... slowly, serene... beneath her agate Pole.
Time is not, when Love pervades all sense;
all things yearn tacitly for *Restoration
Day*; wee Rhodri Everyman shall compass all.
Christ be that rosy wheel : my song is evidence.

11.18.24

82

GOLD FOIL

Hesiod the farmhand, familiar with hardship,
his fallow fields the color of dry straw,
gazes toward Lebanon hills. The sun's a chip
of pale silver. Rasp of a far-off saw,
only a whisper in the silence. Hunger aches.
There be good strife and bad aboard this ship,
he hums. Midas disobeyed that Law,
turning all to gold – root of Man's mistakes.
Harvest is plentiful : but the laborers skip

right down to Sheol, as the Hebrews say.
The Gods of gold and silver have left town;
only dry leaves, like rusted iron, stay –
shattered bronze helmets, Cadmus-sown.
There be good faith and guile, Hesiod croons.
Square root of concord : key to the highway,
he murmurs. Truthfulness, from foot to crown –
this be my Goddess, beyond suns and moons.
Psyche… Sophia… hear my prayer, today.
                                        *

The winter season is upon is now
in Minnesota. I walk the River Road,
my golden hair gone gray, with streaks of snow.
Past Grandpa's house, of brick and limestone
                                        made.
He built grain elevators in Saskatchewan;
listened to Marian Anderson on the radio,
vinyl Maria Callas. Rightness in his head,
sweetness at heart. That Yule log he would burn –
it was himself : his better angel (somehow).

False prophets rise, and sow division;
they would deface the human *Imago*.
Our only hero is the Good Samaritan :
lifting hurt scapegoats, lowest of the low.
Our God's the god of Noah, and Deucalion.
There's but one law of rightness, here below
(illustrated in the parable, my prodigal son).
The heart builds all – with LOVE, beyond reason;
raising life's barn (in her eternal fashion).

*

That smiling person, standing by the pyre
seems neither man nor woman... I don't know.
He feeds me when I'm hungry. Only enquire,
she says. Into the woods, you want to go.
There is a family of tall cedar trees –
seek there for keel, and prow, and spire;
seek there for warmth, for winter's kindling-glow.
Seek there for manger, shepherds at their ease –
for Elijah too, sailing his chariot of fire.

Hesiod tasted the bitter bread of toil.
His poverty darkened his judgement so
he saw no grace... release from sour soil.
Yet his heart was firm – sought justice here below.
The spirit, like a small, snow-crystal,
glints through this wintry cosmos of the whole
vast massive void of galaxies... we go
where Providence ordains. And rise, we shall –
like bread upon a roaring hearth : gold foil.

11.21.24

A REQUIEM

Adagio, more solemn than a requiem,
draws on. November melancholy
stirs my memory. That simple hymn
blind Rev. Gary Davis picked for me
and the other college kids, in 1970 –
sweet Gospel milk-and-honey. *Anthem*
Hendrix played, at Woodstock – *sittin' here*
with your violins, hittin' mild MLK…
striking down Kennedy. A requiem.

Music of the abyss… might *kiss the sky*.
But now the violence comes from within
(not without violence). In the eye's a stye.
Rape, fraud and murder coalesce one din
of sin – blind, callous FORCE its name.
We might not gather on St. Cecilia's Day
to mourn the death of civilization,
snuffing the spirit's candle with your crime –
an airless shame. Children would whimper, *why*?

But that was Providence… and long ago.
My complaining flute, complementary lute…
weak toys, for troubled hearts (so blue).
Neighbors turn mob, a mindless brute –
bruising *Psyche, Liberty, Columbia*.
Old Ironsides is blistered by tornado.
Ark, *Argo* limp on home, by another route.
                              *
He sleeps on a sloop, in Narragansett Bay :
our once and future *Son of Man* (PT-boat boy-o).
                    11.22.24

SHALOM

Rapt up by the Goddess's four horses
toward the fiery ice, the icy fire
of everlasting Truth, Parmenides
was like the rest of us. When hearts retire
from common fellowship with everyone;
forsake the Forum, every public space,
drawn by a dream of wholeness, LOVE entire :
spouse, comrade, *sister-dove*, soul-twin : when
animale compagnevole flames out – like Orpheus

after Eurydice... like David, Jonathan...
like Mary Magdalen, Jesus... Jesus
and John... Dante and Beatrice... (everyone).
Bon feu de joie, no water ever quenches!
Pure flame, horsepower of the sun!
Light's ever-self-refining, silver pin-
point, in the whorling galaxies – Polaris!
Here pilgrim-travails end where they began –
at the far-nearness of the Earth's hearthstone.

*

Vainamonen the smith, that immortal Finn
hammered out with fire his magic *Sampo*-boat :
a floatable dish, a flying saucer-pan –
sound cornucopia, serving each fleet note
with fluted wine, on conch-shell swells.
It was both coracle and hydroplane –
a shield against rage, tohu-bohu... whatevernot
might break the peaceful wonder of his spells.
So let his feast of Finnish harmony begin!

86

And in that *Ocean State*, that microcosm –
haven for Roger Williams, and his friends –
we'll gather by that hearty hearth of welcome
with every refugee from Earth's dead ends;
we'll join all hands above that clambake feast
at the Round Table in Jerusalem
(and Galilee). So Sabbath makes amends,
and speedy sparks fly north, west, south, and east
beneath the wings of *Jonah*-Noah (gliding home).

*

Parmenides was both philosopher and poet –
singing, asking unanswerable questions.
Knew that every word from human lips – about
sky or earth – came from human persons.
In the beginning was the Word – and the Word
of words, like a Person of persons – *fiat*
lux : LIGHT, floating down from far heavens.
And to think it was a person... just felt weird!
He burned his candle over this – all night.

And so it was. It helped to be around
a Round Table, among loving friends.
All faults were forgiven, except one –
against the truth of Truth to raise a hand.
Some hung around there, harboring a lie.
God saved their punishment, until the end
(too late to turn around). Liars blend
into the fabric – yet our hero bends gently
down, to kiss them : farewell, *shalom*, goodbye.

11.23.24

RESTORATION DAY

This autumn season's like a plummet-stone.
The river is a snake of dark-gray lead
slowly gliding to the Gulf. Unknown,
that kid, on some American beachhead
molds his castle – only a clear surmise.
Just a sketch, now. *And so castles made of sand…*
– somehow lifting me, and you. Not blue, not red.
Just colors of plain skin, below grey skies.
With tired hand… (now Leonardo's done).

Reporters were talking to folks in Cloquet,
in the paper today. Limping over the grass
to her soldier's grave, to kneel and pray,
she feels the titanic power, wielded over us
by flickering tongues of arrogant callous men
in Washington. All subtlety is wasted spray
spit across the internet, like poison gas.
Thus propaganda prods the serpents' den.
When trust is past, glib foxes hunt their prey.

Inching, like an injured turtledove,
across the frozen ground, you have become
one of the wingèd ones, drifting down from above
whose glance we might catch, faintly, in a dream.
One of those angels, in an old fresco
whose light still lingers in our dark alcove :
eyes full of pity, mind weighing the sum
of suffering… heart knows, from long before.
Singing : *the balm, for all the evil done, is* LOVE.

Scripture's promise *to restore all things*
has been interpreted in many ways.
Proud lawyers for the Lord attach their strings,
while snooty scribes prevaricate – they glaze
the mind with a prickly haze of weedy thought.
And yet… *the kingdom of God is in your midst*, sings
out that Nazarene *Nazir*. *Men do not see it, hey-
ey-yo*. The telegraph pings – *What hath God wrought?*
News travels fast. (Scorpion bides his stings.)

People feel vaporized. Just an outline,
just a shadow on the wall. Of force.
Of noise. Of course. But you are mine,
sweet *Psyche*… delicate, classical *Grace*.
Athena Strong-Arm – stronger *Mary Magdalen*;
wise sprightly *Sophie*, riding on her horse.
The muse of Benjamin Latrobe – that airy space
above the Dome, above the Globe. *Bee Mine*.

Upon her granite island in the harbor, *Liberty*
still lifts her torch, still hugs her tables
of Learning, of Law – whose root is *Charity*.
Do you know it, heart? Despite these cables
littering each brain, unto distraction?
The ground of *Union* is *Equality*.
Its *mutuality* hoists humankind, from pig-stables
to one bright Round Table : to *Restoration
Day*. I spy old Camelot… there's JFK!

*

The people of Cloquet have spoken. Tough
old Iron Range town, I used to hitchhike through
up to the lake. I didn't care enough
about my notebooks, once – a cold wind blew
and flipped my knapsack right off the bridge,
into St. Louis River (smelly, then – just sniff
the paper mills). Acid ink-spills, blue
and red... and one faint violet image :
small half-moon shade (tall pine tree's trough).

To get to know someone, you have to talk.
Then mental angles shift, like sliding doors...
you sense a careworn heart, walking her walk.
An air of tacit understanding (slight breeze
whispering through these birches, northern
                              spruce).
I'd never vote for that scumbag, the pock-
marked veteran declares. *But these here lawyers
in D.C.... can't tell a farmer from a goose.* Pride
shines vain minds... only to sting, to mock, mock.

St. Louis River flows down to Duluth,
into that great, cold, ocean-going Lake.
Rose-fingered Dawn whispers to me, forsooth :
Ulysses must another journey make.
Grant that all travelers find welcome fire
in this our home, beside our hearth –
we ask this for our good Lord's sake,
who died in pain, under the Roman Empire. And
may his *Turtledove* drift down... to sing, to soothe.

                              11.24.24

90

ASHEN ROSE

This lowly sun of near-December, shot
through ancient window-glass (wavy, groggy)
flickers a tiny rainbow. A little knot
of light – early, ephemeral apogee –
against my annealing wall. A year's farewell.
My lips are murmuring of what is not
yet there... yet all is ready, already :
a nest, is all. *Hamlet would bid adieu,*
Ophelia – come : his look is grave, my tot.

The glinting of some tarnished coin – *écu?*
Penny? – rays as water waves, through streams.
Copper is mossy green; pure iron is blue
and rust is as the faded rose of dreams...
Come come, milord. Enough sad word-play.
Here's a tender avocado, just for you.
That's our moon, amid her jungle creams –
works like a magnet o'er your seasick clay.
Draws out your Iron Age, *with a ruby's hue.*

*

Le mage du Kremlin – image of a Czar –
draws poets, Anna, as despots, to pots of gold.
This magnetism crosses wires, of power
with the heart's desire : watch them infold
unto one fateful sad scarlet carnation.
The unknown soldiers always go before.
They are the pioneers mislaid, forgot
by generation after wayward generation :
brave ones, living and dead, who struggled here.

My grubsy tug, my model *Ironsides* –
glued up by slippery sap of dead horses –
my sagging Uncle Sam, against the tides
of Caesars' raging seizures – alters course
again : *magnetic North*! Your *mandorla*,
my dove, my lodestone Magdalen – abides;
tendre-tristesse, twin wheels into one rose
meld in communion – LOVE's *equalità*;
so *Iris*, through soft rings of showers, glides.

*

A little agate, in the northern spring
whorled like an ice-chip coming to life
or like a moss-green coin, slowly becoming
coppery again (Venusian) – up in Yellowknife
or Itasca, once – you found : your chosen stone.
Four rivers, it was harboring
amid tall cedar arbors. Here the strife
of Man against all men would be undone.
It was a union of grey slate and silver ring –

a rainbow ring : *Jonah*'s deep throaty song
out of the deep. And like that gold *écu*
from Paris, compassing both right and wrong,
both good and bad, to be made new –
in mercy we were reconciled, in LOVE
made one, made whole again. *O hallelu!*
In UNION all the weak grow strong.
In fiery fellowship, borne from above...
by YOU : you ashen ROSE : your living tongue.
11.25.24

GREAT MOON

Full fathom five thy father lies, Phoebe,
Sophie, your grandfather. His eyes are pearls,
his blind wisdom. A prehistoric sea
decalled these limestone duplex walls of ours
on St. Cecilia's Street – where I am buried
now, like Berryman, in Resurrection Cemetery.
Tomorrow is your mother's birthday. Whorls
of shadows, waves of memories, recede…
and rise again : Moon's majestic gravity.

The round world rolls around the sun,
the moon around the earth, her shadow twin.
Antigone was almost buried with Ismene –
like you, stubborn contrarian, with dear Susan
(your sister-twin). My heart's a *matryoshka*,
doll : the seven layers of my onion mind
need peeling away, before conscience is clean
(at the very end). Your under-leaf, *Eurydice-
Hecate* – white willow… (pale, lunar green).

Your round moon-face, reflected in your child,
is ever shadowing my heart : its melancholy
luminosity. Each heart lives in its tacit world,
like Edgar Poe, in poetry – but I remember Emily
as well (as you do, too). *Hope is the anchor
of the soul* : *Hope* is the badge of Little Rhody.
Roger (with Rhodri) in the wheelhouse twirled
twin roses… *heaviness, and tenderness*… right there :
great Moon over Narragansett beams (brave, mild).

11.26.24

www.ingramcontent.com/pod-product-compliance
Lightning Source LLC
Chambersburg PA
CBHW071534120626
46550CB00006B/2459